365

ways to be HAPPY

365 WAYS TO BE HAPPY

An Hachette UK Company
www.hachette.co.uk

Vie Books, an imprint of Summersdale Publishers Ltd
Part of Octopus Publishing Group Limited
Carmelite House
50 Victoria Embankment
LONDON
EC4Y 0DZ
UK

www.summersdale.com

Printed and bound in China

ISBN: 978-1-78783-231-2

Substantial discounts on bulk quantities of Summersdale books are available to corporations, professional associations and other organizations. For details contact general enquiries: telephone: +44 (0) 1243 771107 or email: enquiries@summersdale.com.

365

vie *ways to be* HAPPY

With the rapid pace of modern life, and the ever-increasing demands on us to be better, have more and work harder, we often forget about our mental well-being and how important it is to be happy. Take a proactive and mindful approach to your happiness.

2

Take positive steps each day to make lasting changes and make every step count.

By picking up this book you've made a constructive start in your bid for lasting happiness. You have begun your journey.

4 Find your own path to happiness and follow it.

5 Making happiness your priority is a powerful action. You are worth it.

6 Remember: happiness comes by choice, not by chance.

7

William James, a prominent American psychologist in the nineteenth century, studied happiness and concluded that we choose to be happy…

8

… He theorized that the act of believing that you can be happy will in turn lead to your happiness.

9

Try this: the next time you're
feeling low, reminisce about a time
when you were happy and immerse
yourself in those memories.

Visualize your past self and believe that you
can attain that level of happiness again.

To visualize: find a quiet place and sit comfortably...

... Close your eyes and breathe slowly and deeply. Think of your happy memory and recall the sensory experience.

Visualize the memory from your own perspective, and not as though you were watching a film.

Think like the poet Charles Baudelaire, who said,
"A multitude of small delights constitute happiness."
It really is the little things that are actually the big things,
such as a flower in bloom or a sunny afternoon. Be mindful
of small moments of joy in your day and acknowledge them
when they occur. They will lift your mood for longer.

15

Simple experiences, like the gift of a free afternoon or watching the clouds go by, afford far greater pleasure than attaining material goods.

Rather than hitting the shops when you need a happiness hit, head outside to your nearest green space for some free mood-lifting entertainment!

17

Stand barefoot on grass.

18

Trail your fingers through water.

19

Close your eyes and listen to birdsong.

Talking to a good friend (or friends) about your problems can help you to put your own worries in perspective; equally, congratulating each other on the good things happening in your lives is a wonderful way to boost your happiness levels. Whether you're stuck in a negative spiral or have some good news to share, talk to people around you who can offer you their support.

21

Cultivating mutual respect and support in your friendships is key to positive mental well-being for both you and your loved ones.

22

Laughter releases endorphins, one of the body's "feel good" chemicals. When released, endorphins give you a "buzz", increasing feelings of euphoria and reducing stress. They can even raise your pain threshold!

Never apologize for being you, because you're wonderful just the way you are.

Believe that you deserve happiness.

Spend time with loved ones who make you feel better, not worse.

26

Don't waste time on people who don't
have your best interests at heart.

27

Do not listen to people who
belittle or undermine you.

28

Let go of people in your life who
feed your negative thinking.

29 Get a pen and paper and write down all the things in your life that put a smile on your face, such as spending time with friends.

30 Include your successes, such as skills you've mastered or goals that you've reached. You may surprise yourself with how long the list is. Put this list somewhere where you'll see it every day.

31

Remind yourself that it is your actions
that have brought happiness into your life.
You are the architect of your own joy.

32

Counter every negative thought you have
about yourself with a positive one.

Every week, write down three good things that happen to you – research published in the *Journal of Clinical Psychology* found that those who adopted this habit became significantly happier. This could include...

... Eating a delicious meal.

... Seeing a loved one.

... Making someone laugh – on purpose! Your brain releases feel-good chemicals when you make others happy.

37 ... Arriving somewhere on time, or even early!

38 ... Finding money in your pocket unexpectedly.

39 Nothing is too small to be counted. Moments of happiness come in all shapes and sizes.

40

Give yourself a goal or intention for the day before getting up. It could be something as simple as "stay calm at work".

Don't make it an actual "thing" to do as this may cause anxiety.

41

42

Regularly repeating a mantra to yourself can help you reaffirm your core beliefs. Mantras should express your positive perspective on the world.

43

Create a mood board to help you stay focused on your goals.

44

Put together a board that sparks joy when you look at it.

Start your mood board by gathering together beautiful images of places you want to visit, zingy colours and fabric swatches, and inspiring quotes and snippets of poetry that make you smile every time you read them. Hang your board in a prominent place and keep adding to it as your goals and dreams evolve.

It is very easy to forget your own needs when you lead a busy life, full of responsibilities.

Block out time on your calendar as "me time".

Spend that time just doing the things you enjoy...

... Spend time on your hobbies...

... Catch up with your favourite TV shows...

... Or simply do nothing!

Sit and think, or meditate and appreciate your own company.

52

53

If any intrusive thoughts threaten your peace of mind, simply acknowledge their existence...

... and let them go.

54

A treat can boost your happiness. If you're feeling sad, tense or anxious, do something nice – however small – for yourself.

Tuck into a sumptuous dessert or enjoy a relaxing soak in the bath.

Plan your treat in advance. Having something to look forward to will help you remain positive throughout the day.

57

58

You can even book treats in your diary!

Schedule fun things at regular intervals so that every month is full of bright spots and happy moments.

59

Pick out treats that don't cost money. On sunny days you could organize a ball game...

60

61

... and on colder days, invite friends over for a movie night.

Research local festivals; they often offer a program of free exhibitions and events.

62

Smiling releases endorphins. Even if you don't feel like it, turning up the corners of your mouth into a smile will boost your mood. Recent studies have shown that through the enhancement of positive emotions with facial expressions, a person's mood begins to align with the emotion that their face is communicating, so show those pearly whites!

64

Use this as your mantra when stepping outside: smile and the world will smile back.

See everything with a sense of wonder, like a child seeing something for the first time.

Studies show that you have a greater chance of being happier day-to-day if you actively pursue a pastime.

The feeling of losing yourself in study or creative pursuit is referred to as "flow".

Being in the state of "flow" is, according to some psychologists, where true happiness lies.

69

Steer your life to happiness by asking
yourself some tough questions.

70

Ask yourself: do I know what I want from my life?

71

Am I happy in my work life?
Am I happy in my personal life?

72

If your current situation is making you unhappy then consider what you could change that would make you feel more positive.

73

Set realistic goals that help you feel inspired and excited about making changes – and choose the goals that are right for you, not ones to please anyone else.

74

Write down your aspirations and identify the first steps to achieving them.

75

For example, if you fancy a career change, research your dream field or make an appointment with a careers advisor.

76

Change is within your grasp.

We all have a habit of holding on to negative experiences, guilty feelings, regrets and bad friends. It's time to make a pact with yourself and let those negative things go, so you can move forward to a happier, brighter future. It feels good sometimes to say, "No more!" or "I'm never doing that again!" You can even say these words out loud, to make your decision feel real.

78

Repeat this affirmation in the morning:
yesterday is the past, today is a new day.

79

Remember, whatever has gone before, you can
always take a fresh step into a hopeful future.

80

Don't delay, make your first change here and now.

Revel in what makes you different and unique.

Don't feel under pressure to do
or be what others expect of you.

If you feel conflicted, remember that no one
knows you better than you know yourself.

84

Consider the wise words of the psychologist William Herbert Sheldon: "Happiness is essentially a state of going somewhere, wholeheartedly, one-directionally, without regret or reservation."

85

Stick to your decisions and have the courage of your convictions. It is a sure route to true happiness because you feel in control of your life.

86

Repeat these mantras:
I am responsible for my own happiness...

87

... I am the master of my destiny.

88

Perfection is an impossible goal; striving
for it will deny you the opportunity to feel
good about your achievements.

89

Don't compare yourself to others.
It steers you away from looking at all the
positive things happening in your own life.

90

Don't believe that emulating others will make you
happy; try to be the best version of you and look
at the areas in your life that could be improved
on as well as appreciating what you're good at.

Look to the future with creative visualization.

Start by sitting comfortably, closing your eyes and breathing deeply. Picture a happier, contented you...

... how do you look? Where are you?
Notice every detail and enjoy how it feels.

Sharing joy is a powerful act. The Buddha said,
"An act to make another happy inspires the other to
make still another happy, and so happiness is aroused and
abounds." Studies support this, showing that the good
feeling we get when we witness people helping those
around them inspires us to be altruistic ourselves.

One recent study concluded that those who do good for selfless reasons live longer.

Volunteer your free time by helping out at a local charity or not-for-profit organization.

Altruism is also linked to stronger and happier relationships.

98

Buy a gift for a friend or loved one. Research shows that spending money on other people rather than yourself makes you feel good.

You don't have to spend a lot of money to feel good. Giving a little treat is enough.

99

100

Remember that a joy aired is a joy shared.

101

Telling your friends about your successes can help
you to feel as though your happiness is worth celebrating.

102

Don't worry about "showing off" – true friends
want to hear about your successes.

103

Book a holiday or day out with your friends. Shared experiences are proven to offer greater, longer-lasting happiness as the experiences can be reminisced about.

104

Planning and anticipating a good experience makes us feel positive and happy, so start researching that trip!

105

Even trips that go wrong provide funny memories!

106

Organize a day after the holiday to meet and look over the photos and videos from your trip.

107

Recreate a meal from the trip; everyone can bring a drink or dish.

Write a letter by hand to a friend or relative who lives at the other end of the country. Use this as an opportunity to catch up in a way you wouldn't be able to over the phone or via social media, by being honest and open, without judgement. Ask them plenty of questions.

Include a memento such as a photograph in your letter.

109

110

You may get a reply, which will add to your joy and satisfaction.

111

Host a movie night for a group of friends and don't forget the popcorn!

112

Sing for joy! Singing releases endorphins, so not only does it make you feel happier, but it's also a great stress reliever.

113

The deep breathing required for singing increases oxygen in the blood, so it's good for your health...

... and since it is known to improve your posture,
this too could give you a happiness boost.

It can even tone your tummy!

Joining a choir is even more rewarding
as it's a great way to make friends.

Get in touch at least once a year with
the people that matter most to you.

Send each of your friends a
thoughtful card on their birthday.

A good hug boosts happiness levels, lowers
your blood pressure and reduces stress.

120

Keep in mind that happiness is contagious. Happy people make people happy.

121

Give someone a compliment. Giving or receiving a compliment boosts self-esteem and happiness levels – so make the effort to make someone's day.

As the poet Samuel Taylor Coleridge put it: "The happiness of life is made up of minute fractions – the little, soon forgotten charities of a kiss or smile, a kind look, a heartfelt compliment, and the countless infinitesimals of pleasurable and genial feeling." Show kindness to those around you with genuine feeling. The more positivity you put out in to the world, the more you will receive from others.

123

If you love someone, let them know. It will mean the world to them to hear you say it – just as it will to you, if they reciprocate.

Studies show that speaking to a loved one makes us feel happier.

125 Call up one person a day for a catch-up...

126 ... or message them!

127 It can lift your spirits even on a bad day.

128

Offer to walk a dog for a friend or family member...

129

...You'll give them some free time to themselves...

130

... And you'll have the opportunity to get out into nature and spend time with an animal companion.

131

Stop buying things you don't really
want. When you love what you have,
you have everything you need.

132

Designate "no spend" days
where you make no purchases.

133

If you're not sure about a potential
purchase, wait two weeks.

134

Declutter your home. Having a tidy, clutter-free home is important for general happiness and well-being. Having clear surfaces and a place for everything is calming.

135

The act of tidying can be satisfying too, and the low-impact workout that comes from cleaning produces serotonin.

136

The act of repeating a positive mantra can lower your blood pressure and decrease levels of tension.

137

138

Repeat these mantras:
I deserve happiness...

... I am worthy of good things.
Good things will come to me.

139

Get hygge! Hygge is a Danish word that describes the feeling of being cosy.

140

To be hygge is to be at peace with the world. Sitting in front of a log fire on a winter's night or curling up under a blanket with a favourite book might help you achieve it.

141

Pursue "everyday happiness". Simply taking
the time to enjoy a perfectly brewed cup of coffee
or tea is an act of self-care that will inspire joy.

142

Enjoy the warmth of summer even
when indoors. Arrange a daybed by
a window and bask in the sun.

143

Let go of the clothes that you no longer wear.
Whether you've hung on to a favourite pair of jeans in
the hope that you'll fit in to them one day, or you have a
sentimental attachment to an old T-shirt, there are plenty of
reasons you may have a wardrobe that's completely stuffed.
Declutter for a cleaner, calmer home environment.

144

Sell your unwanted clothes online to earn yourself a bit of extra money or donate them to charity.

145

If you're unsure on what you want to get rid of then ask yourself these questions as you're sorting through...

... Do I really love it?

... Do I ever wear it?

... Is it itchy or uncomfortable to wear?

149

Once you've decluttered your wardrobe,
tackle the rest of your home!

150

Clear out your kitchen cabinets...

151

... say goodbye to all of those kitchen
gadgets that are collecting dust.

152

Dispose of all expired and old cosmetics and lotions.

153

Empty your shed.

154

Or even your handbag!

155

Don't take yourself too seriously – learn to laugh at yourself.

156

Admit your failures and own them.

157

Remember, everyone stumbles sometimes. Don't judge yourself too harshly.

158

Avoid financial stress by cutting unnecessary expense.

159

Review your media subscription services
and cancel any that you don't use regularly.

160

Set a takeaway food and drink budget and stick to it.

If you're leaving bank statements and bills unopened because of the fear of what lies within, then it's time to get organized and wise up to your finances for your sanity and long-term happiness. Being in control of your spending will help you feel empowered.

162 Create a spreadsheet of your monthly income and expenditure.

163 Study the spreadsheet and identify where you're overspending.

164 Build a monthly budget and stick to it. You'll know how much money you have left every month, reducing financial uncertainty.

165

Learn to unplug. Shake up your evening routine and implement a "screen ban" two days a week.

166

Studies show that reduced screen time can help prevent headaches and improve sleep quality.

167

Instead of watching TV, make time for hobbies you enjoy or see your friends and loved ones.

Go green. Whether you have a garden or a spare windowsill, tending plants has many health benefits. There's always room for a plant or two!

Having plants in your home has many positive effects, including lower anxiety levels and blood pressure, resulting in you feeling calmer and more optimistic.

170

Think positive. As the writer Ralph Waldo Emerson said, "Nothing great was ever achieved without enthusiasm."

171

Choose to find the upside in doing chores, such as using the time to listen to a podcast or raise your heartrate.

Play music and sing loudly while cleaning.

72

73

Studies show that listening to music while doing chores makes you feel happy.

Unfinished tasks can hang over our heads. Take five minutes now to complete a chore.

74

The cartoonist Charles M. Schulz once said, "Happiness is a warm puppy." Cuddle a friendly dog.

T75

T76

Consider the possibility of getting a pet (ideally from a rescue centre) if you can make the commitment, or just spend time with the pets of your friends or family.

A recent survey found that pet owners generally enjoyed greater levels of self-esteem than those without pets.

T77

Make time for play and do something silly just for fun.

**Go for a walk outside and jump
and kick all the fallen leaves.**

Find a green space and enjoy it as if you were a
child by running, jumping and rolling around.

As adults we often feel that we should spend all of our time being productive and neglect to schedule in downtime. As the author Marthe Troly-Curtin said, "Time you enjoy wasting is not wasted time." Dedicate a whole day to play and don't feel guilty about it.

182

Playing can be simple moments of silliness such as folding junk mail into a paper aeroplane...

183

... or you can go as big as possible. Turn your entire home into a blanket fort!

184

There are even organized events for adults: look online for "make and do" evenings.

185

If you're struggling with feeling guilty about playing then schedule "play time" into your diary as a weekly event.

186

Scheduled play time may sound counter-intuitive but treating fun as a non-negotiable appointment will help you treat it as a priority for maintaining your emotional well-being.

187

If you sleep well, you feel well.
Tackle your bad sleep habits.

188

Open your bedroom window for a period
each day. This will help freshen the scent of
the room and improve the air quality.

189

Declutter your bedroom, especially your
bed and the table and floor by your bed.

Regularly change the bedding. Clean, fresh linen feels luxurious and is healthy for your skin.

Opt for soft lighting, and try not to have screens in the room – that includes TVs, tablets, laptops and phones – as using these before bedtime makes it difficult to sleep.

192

Only keep pictures and knick-knacks that bring you joy by your bedside.

193

Chamomile and lavender scents promote relaxation and will help you sleep. Diffuse these scents as part of your bedtime routine.

194

Treat your bedroom as a sanctuary and only use it for sleep and sex.

195

Donate that ugly picture or knick-knack
– even if a beloved auntie gave it to you!

196

Make your bed in the mornings. This simple task
will keep your linens fresh and comfortable and
make your bed more inviting in the evening.

People react differently to different fabrics –
check your bed sheets are right for you.

**Try natural fabrics – synthetic fabrics can
cause people to overheat and sweat.**

Wash your pillows every three months
and your duvet every six months.

200

One of the most common factors in sleep deprivation is worry. It's important to clear your mind of negative thoughts before you go to bed. Think of three good things that happened to you in the day to banish negative thoughts and go to bed with a positive frame of mind.

201

If you're plagued by worries before sleep then write down what's on your mind.

202

You could even compile a to-do list for the next day so you know you are in control.

203

If you're still struggling, talk to a friend or loved one who can put things into perspective.

204

Add a splash of colour to your bedroom. Bright colours are proven to make you feel more positive and happy.

205

Paint one wall a jaunty colour or, for a less permanent option, buy a brightly coloured throw or colourful painting.

206

Take time to do what makes your soul happy...

207

... Whatever that might involve!

208

Ignore social pressure to conform. As long as
you're not hurting anyone, you're OK!

209

Prioritize your happiness at work. Most of us spend more of our waking hours at work than we do at home.

210

Make friends at work. Having a workmate to chat to during breaks can make your day much happier, and more fun!

211

Suggest a group of you go out for lunch so you can get to know each other.

212

You could even organize an after-work activity such as going to the cinema...

213

... you'll spend time together and have something to talk about at work!

214

Take the time to thank people when they have done a good job – it will spread a happy vibe around the office.

215

The Roman philosopher Seneca said, "Associate with people who are likely to improve you." Seek out colleagues who challenge you to be better.

Don't multitask. According to research, multitasking is destructive to a person's creativity and concentration levels.

Instead of juggling lots of tasks, create a list of priorities and focus on one job at a time.

If you're unconvinced, remember that multitasking is proven to waste more time than it saves.

Avoid second-hand stress from your colleagues.
When a colleague is strained, you can unconsciously absorb
their negativity. Try to offer some positive advice when
they are talking about their problems. If you find that
their behaviour is having a negative impact on your mood,
it's often best to take yourself out of the situation.

Have this as your mantra:
keep calm and stay positive.

220

221

Be mindful that you have chosen
to be positive and happy.

Snack healthily. Sugary treats can
give you a boost but after the rush is
over you can feel low and sluggish.

222

223

Healthy snack options include fresh fruit, nuts and popcorn. These treats will help maintain energy levels and a healthy mind and body.

Stretch regularly to counteract the negative effects of working at a computer all day, such as eye strain or headaches.

224

225

Get outside and take a short walk...

226

... or you could even run up and down stairs!

227

Physical activity will release endorphins
which will boost your positive energy.

Just think: every job should contain an element of fun!

You can lighten even the most mundane tasks by inventing silly games or riddles such as awarding yourself points for every task you complete...

... then tally your points at the end of your day and award yourself achievements, such as "email master" or "data-entry destroyer".

231

Even if you can't make these certain aspects of your job fun, you can spice up your daily routine.

232

If you have a demanding task that requires a lot of mental focus, try doing something simple with your hands at the same time – such as making a paperclip chain.

Think of being happy as one of your responsibilities at work. Scottish writer Robert Louis Stevenson said, "There is no duty we so much underrate as the duty of being made happy." Job satisfaction doesn't just improve your day but makes you a more productive, creative and loyal worker. You deserve to be happy for your own sake but it will also help your career!

Learn to say "no" at work. This can be daunting but it is good professional conduct to know your limits.

234

235

Practise politely declining in front of a mirror if you need to.

Think of saying "no" as providing useful feedback to your superiors on your workload.

236

Saying "yes" when you can't take on more tasks may raise your stress levels and negatively impact your work.

237

238

It's OK if you realize that you've taken too much on. Talk to your superior...

... you can always delegate!

239

240

Keep your desk and your desktop tidy.
A tidy workplace means that you can
get on with your job without constantly
trying to find misplaced items.

241

Delete old files and pictures, and be
vigilant with your downloads folder and
recycling bin as these can get cluttered.

242

Practise good desktop hygiene and ensure every file is sorted into a labelled folder.

243

Schedule time every week to check that every file is where it ought to be.

244

Keep an archive folder for obsolete records.

245

Take a break. It's important to take your holiday entitlement. Everyone needs time away to de-stress and recharge. Taking a break is proven to make us healthier in general and more productive in the workplace, so don't feel guilty about booking those two weeks off!

246

Choosing the right foods is an important step toward lasting happiness. There are ten key nutrients that combat low mood...

247

Up your calcium intake to help reduce mood swings and even reduce anxiety. Consume calcium with fat to help your body process it more effectively.

248

Calcium is found in dairy products such as milk or cheese...

249

... in nuts such as almonds...

... or leafy greens such as kale, cabbage and spinach.

250

251

Chromium helps the brain to regulate moods...

252

... a lack of chromium can lead to an increased risk of depression.

Chromium can be found in broccoli, turkey, potatoes and wholegrain products.

253

254

A deficiency of folate (also known as folic acid or vitamin B9) can lead to anaemia.

255

Folate deficiency anaemia can lead to weakness, irritability, heart palpitations and headaches.

256

Folate-rich foods include lentils, kidney beans, asparagus, eggs, beets, citrus fruits, kale and Brussel sprouts.

257

Iron transports oxygen around the body and strengthens muscle. Depleted levels lead to fatigue, low mood and depression. Iron deficiency is more common in women.

Find iron in red meat, fish, beans, pulses, nuts, wholegrain products and dark-green leafy vegetables such as kale.

258

259

Magnesium plays an important role in the body's production of serotonin, a mood-balancing chemical.

260

Serotonin deficiency can lead to a predisposition to stress and irritability.

261

Magnesium is present in nuts, leafy greens and fish.

262

Omega–3 fatty acids help your cells to function optimally and a deficiency can lead to depression.

263

**There are three omega-3 fatty acids.
ALA can be found in canola and flax seed.**

264

Omega-3s EPA and DH can be found in seafood such as mackerel, herring, salmon and oysters, or algal oil (which is vegan).

265

Vitamin B6 is important in the creation of neurotransmitters, which are the chemicals the body uses to regulate emotions.

Foods that are rich in vitamin B6 include pork, eggs, soya beans, bananas, avocados, chicken, brown rice and spinach.

266

267

A vitamin B12 deficiency can lead to extreme tiredness and mental fog.

268

The body struggles to absorb B12 from food so supplements can help bolster your levels.

Find vitamin B12 in fortified cereals, eggs, marmite, chicken and salmon.

269

270

Vitamin D helps the body produce serotonin, one of its feel-good chemicals. People who don't get enough vitamin D can experience low moods. As one of the main sources of vitamin D is sunlight, people are especially at risk of deficiency during the cloudy winter months, causing "winter blues". Try a light-therapy lamp; this imitates natural sunlight and can prevent a drop in serotonin production. Or consider taking a daily vitamin D supplement.

271

Zinc is a great mood balancer and is known
to reduce symptoms of depression.

272

It can be found in mushrooms,
eggs, chickpeas and lentils...

273

... or red meat such as beef or lamb
or seafood such as oysters.

274

Feed your thyroid. This gland in your neck produces and stores hormones that affect the function of almost every cell in your body. Thyroid problems are linked to mood swings and depression.

275

Eat iodine-rich fish and eggs, drink chamomile tea, and ensure your diet contains enough vitamins A and D to give your thyroid what it needs to make you feel good.

Go nuts to get happy. When eaten in moderation, nuts provide protein, fibre, healthy fats and plenty of other vitamins and minerals that keep your body in perky condition.

276

277

Eat two Brazil nuts a day for your daily dose of selenium.

Selenium is essential for your bodily well-being – it's an antioxidant that reduces the risk of cancer, and it's also needed for a healthy immune system.

278

279

Follow a low-GI diet to help regulate your mood. GI stands for glycaemic index: the ranking of carbohydrate-containing foods based on their overall effect on blood glucose levels. Eating foods with a high GI, such as white bread, pastries and sweets, causes our blood sugar to spike and rapidly drop, leaving us tired, irritable and hungry.

280

Low-GI foods include beans, rye bread
and most fruit and veg. Eat these to avoid
spikes and dips in your blood sugar.

281

Water carries nutrients to our
body's cells and flushes the toxins out.
Drink six to eight glasses of water a day
to promote well-being and happiness.

282

Stay hydrated; dehydration leads to confusion and irritability.

283

Hot drinks count toward your daily water intake.

284

Fruit juices and fresh vegetables also contain enough water to hydrate you.

285

Cut out caffeine from your diet.

286

Or reduce it: more than nine cups of coffee a day
can cause extreme stress and panic attacks.

287

Swap out breakfast tea for herbal teas:
caffeine inhibits the body's receptors of adenosine
– a natural sedative that keeps us calm.

288

Try chamomile tea. A recent study showed that participants who drunk chamomile tea for two weeks experienced fewer symptoms of depression.

Drink sage tea. Sage consumption has been linked to improved mental function and mood. Studies have also shown lemon balm tea to have similar effects.

289

290

Cut back on the booze, even
if it's been a stressful day.

291

Try a non-alcoholic beer to enjoy
the taste without side-effects.

292

If you do drink alcohol, opt for a glass of
Merlot as the grape skins used in this wine
are rich in the sleep hormone melatonin.

293 Set a budget before you go for a night out so you limit your alcohol intake.

294 Alternate alcoholic drinks with water, so you feel well hydrated and don't overload on costly booze.

295 Cut down little by little. It is easier to change your habits in small increments and you can track your progress.

296

Swap out the starchy goods for wholegrains to stabilize your energy levels. Replace white bread with wholemeal and white rice with brown rice.

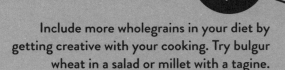

297

Include more wholegrains in your diet by getting creative with your cooking. Try bulgur wheat in a salad or millet with a tagine.

298

Boost your mood with maca. Maca powder is a superfood made from the maca plant, which grows in the Peruvian Andes. It's particularly good for women who suffer from PMT and low mood, relieving anxiety, depression and general aches and pains. Try it sprinkled onto cereal or added to smoothies or baked goods.

299

Take up swimming for a
low-impact exercise option.

300

If possible, walk to your destination instead
of taking another form of transport.

301

Try one of the many free exercise
videos available online.

302

Research says just 20 minutes of exercise can boost your mood for up to 12 hours. Exercise releases endorphins and dopamine, the brain's "happy" chemicals.

If you're struggling to get motivated to do some exercise, try pairing up with a friend and attending a class.

303

304

Exercising with others can help you stay motivated; try joining a class or team.

305

Take up a new and exciting form of exercise like rock climbing.

306

You could even rediscover an old favourite that you enjoyed at school.

Get up early. The writer Henry David Thoreau said,
"An early-morning walk is a blessing for the whole day."

Get outside and enjoy the fresh air. Studies show that people
have a happier outlook if they spend time in nature.

309

Take a deep breath to increase the
amount of oxygen in your body.

310

Higher oxygen levels leads to a clearer
mind and more energy, so breathe in!

311

Sign up to an outdoor exercise class
such as yoga in the park.

312

Listen to music while you exercise. Studies have shown that listening to high-energy music while exercising boosts your mood and makes the workout seem easier.

313

If you can, watch a show while you work out. It will make the time go quicker and take your mind off the discomfort!

314

Practise yoga; you will strengthen your body and balance your mood.

315

Download an app to access short yoga workouts on the go.

316

Stay for the yogic sleep at the end of the class; you will feel refreshed.

Incorporate more lean proteins such as chicken, fish and tofu into your diet. They keep you feeling full for longer and contain amino acids, which help your body to produce serotonin, dopamine and noradrenaline which in turn balance your mood and make you feel more positive.

318

Try wild swimming in a lake or the sea to experience nature while exercising. The endorphin high from wild swimming makes you happy and ready to take on life's challenges.

319

Go forest bathing. Originating in Japan, where it is known as *shinrin-yoku*, forest bathing is the practice of immersing yourself in the woods or forest.

320

Walk through a forest and engage all of your senses. Clear your mind and focus on the here and now.

321

Turn your face to the sky and enjoy the sunlight dappling your skin.

322

Press your palms against a tree trunk and close your eyes.

323

Embark on a guided nature walk. Your guide will help you identify points of great natural beauty.

324

Try a foraging course and learn about nature's bounty.

325

Go rock pooling between spring and early autumn. Wonder at the remarkable diversity of marine life.

Try to connect with nature every day and enjoy the positive effects on your health and happiness – it could be something as simple as walking through autumn leaves and listening to the crunching sound they make, stopping to smell a beautiful flower or hugging an ancient oak tree. You may have to look a bit harder for nature if you're in an urban area but you can do it! Most cities have designated green spaces available to the public. You could even keep an eye out for urban allotments or window boxes and hanging baskets.

327

When you feel your happiness levels start to drop, try complementary therapies such as meditation to give yourself a positive boost.

328

Search online for a guided meditation video to help you get started or attend a class run by a local practitioner.

329

Meditate daily. Brain scans have shown that
Buddhist monks, who practise regular meditation,
have happiness levels that are off the charts.
Studies have shown that those who meditate for
10 minutes a day sleep better, are happier and are
more resilient when it comes to handling stress.

Try these different forms
of meditation to see
what works for you:

330

331

Mettā meditation promotes feelings
of kindness for yourself and others.

Body scan meditation helps you
recognize and release tension.

332

333

Mindfulness meditation can help practitioners break negative thought cycles. Mindfulness is the act of focusing one's attention on the here and now.

334

Breath awareness meditation is a kind of mindful meditation. The practitioner focuses only on breathing. This can reduce anxiety levels.

335

Kundalini yoga is a physical form of meditation that combines deep breathing and movement to achieve mental well-being.

336

Don't let negative thoughts intrude on your meditative practice. Acknowledge their presence and then let them go, returning your mind to stillness and peace.

337

Mindfulness can be practised at any time, not just during meditation. Find a quiet area and take notice of the details around you, staying focused on the here and now.

338

Practise mindfulness while out and about. Notice the sights, smells and sounds surrounding you.

339

You can be mindful in the home too. Engage your mind when preparing your meals for a rich sensory experience.

340

Introduce mindfulness to your morning routine. Take five minutes to be present in the moment before starting your day.

341

Use this as your morning mantra: one positive thought in the morning can change your whole day.

342

Say your mantra out loud to affirm your words. If you're not sure where to start, try these positive mantras...

343

... I think big and I dream bigger.

344

... My happiness radiates like the sun.

345

... I am open to new experiences. I welcome change.

346

Affirmations are positive phrases that are personal to you. They are short statements that express what we know or wish to be true. Repeat your affirmations in front of a mirror in the morning.

347

Write your affirmations on brightly coloured paper and display them prominently. On the following page are some affirmations to get you started.

I deserve all of the good
things that happen to me.

348

349

I am becoming the
best version of myself.

I am powerful and resilient.

350

35

Laugh out loud. Laughter is good for you; not only does it release endorphins which make you feel happy, but there are proven health benefits too. A good belly laugh is akin to a mild workout session, because it gets the blood flowing and the muscles working. It also reduces stress hormones, lowers blood pressure and gives your immune system a boost.

352

Where appropriate, see the funny side of a situation.

353

Recount a funny situation to a friend – reliving the memory will give your friend a boost too!

354

Spend some time with people who make you laugh.

Sign up to daily funny emails or a newsletter from your favourite comedian, and make a habit of regularly reading comic novels.

355

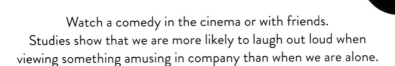

356

Watch a comedy in the cinema or with friends.
Studies show that we are more likely to laugh out loud when
viewing something amusing in company than when we are alone.

357

Host an open-mic night at home and invite your friends.

358

Watch cute animal videos online –
studies show that they reduce stress!

359

Take a break from self-improvement if you're feeling overwhelmed. Rest is crucial to your well-being.

360

Don't worry if you feel like you're letting things slide. As the poet Guillaume Apollinaire said, "Now and then it's important to pause in our pursuit of happiness and just be happy."

361

Keep a success journal. It's important
to celebrate your achievements.

Create a "have done" list instead of a "to-do" list.

363

Every day, list three things you feel grateful for.

Congratulate yourself on your progress, out loud.

364

If your low mood is having a negative effect
on your day-to-day life, it is worth booking an
appointment with your doctor to talk about it.
Although complementary therapies can help,
some situations need medical help. We hope you
enjoy the journey toward a new, happier you!

If you're interested in finding out more about our books, find us on Facebook at **Summersdale Publishers** and follow us on Twitter at **@Summersdale**.

www.summersdale.com